BY THI

OF

THE LITTLE RIVER

To Nancy,
may you walk
in Beauty!
Teal

Poems by

Teal Willoughby

Cover Photo by Stan Rushing

To my parents,

Arline and Charles Teal

Dear Mom,
   I bought this book, thinking of you.
The author is a mom, a Christian,
and a poet. She reminds me of you!
I had her autograph the book for
you and tell me more about the
poems inside. Then I took and
wrote notes to share with you. I
hope you enjoy them!
                    Love,
                    Bree

Table of Contents

BY THE WATERS

OF

THE LITTLE RIVER

Poems by

Teal Willoughby

DOORWAY

I sit in the doorway
cross-legged
where the dog
likes to lie
voices inside discuss
serious issues
but no one asks
any questions why

       Behind me the sun
       plays in the yard
       sneaks past the trees
       and tags me
       on the back
       but I do not answer
       I sit in the doorway
       cross-legged
       between the worlds
       silent
       beholding

OUR LOVE FLOWS

Our love flows from
an invisible fountain
Below the rocks and clay
in this Appalachian hillside,
A bubbling brook
breaking and tearing
Up our body souls

What else to do
with the damage
But laugh at
our soggy clothes
And the bright reddish
thing emerging in
Our chest

My favorite
memories are
being in nature
with Jon and
the girls.

RED BUD TREE

Red bud tree, Red bud tree
      Do you wonder
the cold sleet
drip, drip, dripping
down your naked arms?

Red bud tree, Red bud tree
      Do you wonder
when warm breezes blow
caress your slender body
hug you round and round?

Red bud tree, Red bud tree
      Do you wonder
why the new purple dress and
satin ribbons tied in your hair
dressed up to dance?

Red bud tree, Red bud tree
      Do you trust
the fleshing of your frozen heart
will correspond exactly with
the drama of dark earth and yellow skies?

      Teach me, faith
Red bud tree, Red bud tree

MY HIKING BOOTS

Here are my old hiking boots
        bought on a whim
when walking in the world
        meant pampers and umbrella stroller
slapping together bologna sandwiches
with little feet standing on mine
going in circles most of the day
        from kitchen to crib
and maybe to the store

These boots were kept nearby
    behind the toy chest
        as a prayer of hope
Someday I'll wear them
and hike in a far off woods
        beyond my city
Not like a mother bear with her
        cubs constantly in view
No, I'll take my boots
and lace them up
        Over socks that fit
not forgotten in the dryer
And I'll be slim and my bra
        will fit too!
I will walk with my hands free
and climb rocks for my curiosity

I think of you raising five children! I don't know how you did it, and did it so well!

4

And look out to horizons
I can't imagine now
      I will ask questions
impossible to ask now
and I might stay hiking
      All day long
with no thought for lunch
or naps
No, I won't be like a mother bear
      with her cubs
I will be like the antelope
Aware of only the dirt
beneath my boots
As I go leaping
      through the trees!

I wonder... how could I not always feel like a mother bear?

5

MOUNTAIN GIRL

Are you a mountain girl?
stepping out of air-conditioned car
eyes alert and body tense
walking through the pines to the river

I feel a fear unknown in the city
could I step on a snake?
what lives in these holes on the bank
only silence answers back

I try to recall my carefree youth
when I skipped barefooted
on this old red clay
knew every rock and tree root
my companions in my play

I tell myself I belong
this is my land
I can do what I want
but my heart feels no superiority

Sitting still beside the river
sights and smells grow more familiar
as ants weave around the obstacle of my foot
and the wind lifts gently off the water

Am I a mountain girl?
not a privilege of mere birth
I left these hills and woods long ago
their acquaintance must be made again

So many people and events
the decades far away
can I expect the waters
to remain still and the pines
wait for anyone's return?

So please tell me your intricate story
while I begin the tale of mine
perhaps a camaraderie may bloom
between older pals with worldly wounds ---
            to care for one another

I love this one! The
author said the last
stanza is her
speaking to nature.

7

MOON SPY

Moon smiles at me
as I opened my eyes
this morning
Still on my pillow

Big wide and toothless grin
I saw you Moon
Peeping in
my bedroom window

What were you doing
Hanging out in
that small square
Across from my bed

When your favorite thing
swimming across
the big night sky
Lap after lap

Did you forget your schedule
yours is the graveyard shift
and daytime is naptime
rest and relax

Why this smile

First thing this morning
I know you don't smile
all the time!

Oh, Moon, I don't know
Why this visitation today
with such delightful cheer
but you have gotten my attention!

Please forgive me if
I should perhaps
Spy on you ---
Night and day!

At My Desk

Visions of dazzling light
God walks on water
or turns it into wine
Yes, I believe in miracles
but today in my office
I'm content to sit
with a smaller God
who shrinks so tiny
That the tick of my clock
is marking out sacred time
as I do my paper work
Here at my desk,
my desk
my desk
my desk . . .

The author said this poem is about how we can connect to God, even in the tiniest way.

10

SKINNED ALIVE

I am being skinned,
Skinned alive
except it doesn't hurt,
layer after layer
scraped off
by sheer Beauty ---
almost daily
when I least suspect
Something grabs hold
as I go about my business
Stripping me of
my identity
and what I know
and who I know
and where I've been
Beauty is undoing me!
I shiver and shake
like a dog coming out
of the spring rain,
another layer of the past
Released and gone away
as Beauty sends me off
in a new direction
            Delightfully
                    Unknown

LONG TO MELT

I long to melt
under your hand
like a cube of ice
releasing its form
wet drop by drop
a puddle in your hand
running through your fingers
Yours not mine
and bliss would follow
except the laws of nature
will not be mocked
not by me or anyone
for liquid in hot hands
soon evaporates
Gone, vanished
somewhere in thin air
the task is mine
to search for me
a fearsome journey
Much work
to regain my form
revive my legs
to walk upright
on this earth
Where I belong

HOPE

In proper Buddha mind
I release my fistful
of acorn nuts
over the bridge rail
each potential
falling, falling down
into the swift depth
Gone

Before I step away
up came the bird
the Great Blue Heron
rises on stretched wings
I blink in disbelief
I leave the river
looking up
through oak tree leaves
Shimmering

BY THE WATERS OF THE LITTLE RIVER

I came to know thee
  in summertime
When your treetops
  were thick with leaves
And your waters flowed
  gentle and warm,
We sat together
  late into the evening
Drunk on cricket rhythms
  and firefly light shows
The long summer days
  changed into the season of colors
And I came to know thee
  agitated most of the day
Temper tantrums of red and orange
  shaking me up
I stood among the flying leaves in wonder
  at your fierceness in my face
My pleas for peace
  washed down the river

Now the trees are bare
  Little River cold steel silver
With not much daylight
  to know thee in winter

I long to know thee
But it takes more effort
   coat-hat-boots
I pace back and forth
   along the river bank
Wishing I could experience
   whatever it is
Thus it is my loss
   I'm such a sissy
I turn and run back to the house

I dream of knowing thee
   in springtime resurrection,
I have high expectations
   (if winter prepares me)
Because I so hope by spring
   I will run into your arms
And abandon all!

BLUE MOON IN DECEMBER

Blue Moon in December
Snow clouds wipe your face
Shining it bright and cold,
You surprise me
I see my reflection
in your face
For I am round and fat
like you, sister, and
Splashes of blue rouge
color my cheeks too,
I see you
Peeking over the white veil
That swirls between us
Can you see me
like I see you?
Are you enjoying
Wet kisses of frost
for New Year's Eve
just like me?
or are you all alone
Spying on your sister Earth
Enticing me to visit you again,
Blue Moon in December

WHEN I'M SICK IN BED

When I'm sick in bed
>> You, Divine Lover,
>> You are the center of my life

When I doubt decisions today
>> You are the center of my life

When I feel stupid and small
>> You are the center of my life

When I wonder if I'll ever feel good again
>> You are the center of my life

When I cry with helplessness
>> You are the center of my life

When I long for your wide angle hope
>> You are the center of my life

When I breathe in your loving essence
>> You are the center of my life

When I trust your wisdom is gentle
>> You are the center of my life

When I turn my focus onto you
>> You are the center of my life

When I get up and go on
>> You, Divine Lover,
>> You are the center of my life

BUGLING ELK HERD

We took a hike
on my husband's birthday
To Hatfield Knob
in hope of seeing the
Bugling elk in rut,
Success!
Photos of six elk
plus a close-up video of a bull
bugling to his sweet eye-rolling cow
we headed down the trail then
(quite satisfied)

The elk however weren't finished
for the day
Our success quite ignored
after all it was
human success
That caused their extinction by 1865
when settlers came to
their breeding grounds with
Guns and hunger and desire

Perhaps an instinct triggered
"it's safe now"
on cue the elk herd of 30 or more
Appeared out of the woody thicket

Just as we decided to go back to
take one more look
(not quite satisfied)

We witnessed the herd
claiming the whole open field
Young ones leaping in a wide circle
going faster and faster until
barely touching the earth
And the big bugling bulls'
high pitched song
joined with their stomping of hooves
and shaking of antlers
To signal the cows
who decide to go
Trotting away in the opposite directions
but not as fast as they thought!
The whole field alive and spinning
with the elk's dance of joy
Born once again
on this their Tennessee homeland
Hatfield Knob!
(revelation: it's not about me)

BROWN RIVER SNAKE

A brown river snake
Sits on my log
    my favorite log
Curled up relaxing
    I suppose
I throw a rock
    small rock
Just to wake him up
    (I think it's a male)
Don't get too comfortable
    on my log!
He doesn't move
    (why not?)
The rock bounces plop in the water
    surely he must be dead!

How could he not respond
    to my advances
I move closer
    and closer
Telling myself he's dead
    No reason to fear
I pick up a stick
    a short stick it was
I reach out to remove him
    He slips into the water

I scream and jump back
               dark hatred fills me
That snake
      Tricked me
          Playing dead
             Egging me on
                Choosing my log!

     This is an evil snake
     Straight from Eden
     Right here on my river!
     Destroy him!

What if . . . this brown snake
     is not sending me a personal message
        or responding to who I am
        or what I feel or value

     But a creature
     Created with life and
     Deep instinctual power
     Untapped and unknown by me

     The question
        to my murderous heart
        toward such unknown forces
        who threaten my happy world
Is there room for us both
        on this our riverbank?

MAY ALL THE LONELY

May all the lonely
Wake up today
  and shake off the
Shortsightedness of grief!

May the dawn light
Penetrate these eyelids
  with just enough spark
To begin their work day
Looking out
  instead of down

On the streets of the city,
May the lonely
Bound by a shrill impatience
  of speed and noise
See anew their fellow by passers

Hurrying with their purses and packs
  in all different directions
  To early appointments
Their shared plight
On the sidewalk maze
  Stop, turn, yield

Today as they pass each other
Let their hearts open just a crack
   so a little grief escapes,
Let their gripping fists soften
into a hand
  a hand reaching out
        another hand receiving
and eyes look into eyes
        Seeing people
Not blank figures
        From one face to the next,
Do I hear giggling?
        such a silly fantasy
as we spin into
   The Great Unknown
on our blue and green planet
        Together!

I feel most connected to God when I connect to other people. That's why I like the message of this poem.

I LAY MY HEAD

I lay my head down
  on his heavenly chest
with ear pressed against
  his beating heart
and I hear the groaning
  of the helpless masses
Cries of misery
  too deep to speak
but this sorrow is dispensed
   because within the sounding clamor
is the constant rhythm
  of his merciful heart
beating the monotone of hope ---
                   You are mine
                   You are mine
                   You are mine

MOUNTAIN TOP EXPERIENCE

A time for nakedness
on the blessed mountain top
When truth rains down hard
on the holy Round,
      Our body is freed
and eyes are washed clean
All is transparent
Gloriously
      Connected
but very soon,
      too soon
we will descend
Into the valley of worlds
      If we dress up
with our gold rings
      titles and hats
We humans
(taught by the Jesus how)
can dance it out:
      the rain and the Round
with the truth and the holy
Spirit/body connection
      embracing
Mountain top experience
Swirling in the valley
      Blessing us all

25

TOGETHER ONE

Kiss my red eyes
massage this old neck
     and its bulging disks
Oh, caress my pain away!
place your sweet head
on my worn out heart
Hear my longing
     for your love gaze,
and if you please
embrace this dog-tired body
that's fighting a good fight
     still
tell it how beautiful
     this body will be
Glorious
     Wonderful
          Almighty
Beholding Thee
forever everlasting
     Together One!

KICK AND SPLASH

I want to feel it
    dripping down my hair
I want to kick and splash
And turn a hundred somersaults
    just to get dizzy
Then after I wear myself out
I want to lean back
    my tired body
    floating on top
Relaxed, calm and secure
    as if in my own bed
I close my eyes
    and sleep so sweetly
In the womb of God

    When I wake up
Really wide awake and
Very sober
I call out to
    all who can hear
"We are born from
      womb to womb!"
And the sound of my voice
Echoes back to me
Ever in the womb of God

SMALL ME

I'm so small
I am shrinking
and shrinking more
Tiny little circle
Can this be me?

I lost my arms
with nothing to reach for
Then my legs
Nowhere I want to go,
I shrink smaller
my hands are still
I do not grab
Cling or claim,
I am so small
my feet disappear
when I choose no stands
Can this be me?

I'm a circle
very still
settling down
Slowing
Ideas go by
too little
to house them

they fly onward
Breathe
Be
It's okay,
Simply small
me

I didn't understand
this one! But the
author said it is
about a moment she
had floating in the
ocean. She felt
calm and at peace.

I SEARCH FOR HER

I search for her
　Mother of God
Divine inspiration
　Source of the Godhead
Hidden in the deep dark
　Pregnant with all possibilities
That grow in secret
　Under her beating heart
Flowing out to give
　Giving, giving, giving
Until the Word is transformed
　Into a body that is Life
And it expands within her
　Filling her, Mother of God

The silent joy
　That is hers alone
We cannot imagine
　But in her wisdom
She knows she must let go
　As the birthing of God
Is never stagnant

So with a selfless scream
　She pushes him onward
Into the bright light of day

And he hurries on
Miracles to perform
   Disciples to choose
Places to go

Yes, for his life and sacrifice
   I am eternally thankful
Don't misunderstand me
   Except this one thing,
He never returned
   To kiss her feet
And praise her
   And it has made my journey
Almost impossible
   To find my way back home
Back home to her

ZEN MEDITATION

I face the wall
to find my reflection
breath by breath I count
hoping so for something
       but the wall remains flat

Around and 'round my counting goes
to achieve ten means to begin at one,
while old stories repeat
blurring my vision
       and the wall remains flat

Again I begin with great effort
somewhere between 3 and 4
I think of you,
you or me, does it matter?
       and the wall remains flat

My thoughts going deeper
into circling labyrinths that trap
I must open just one more door
my focus gone
       and the wall remains flat

Icy fingers of emotion tickle up
fantasies of you and me

the counting lost, I begin again
what else to do?
        and the wall remains flat

Then between two breaths
the hope and the fear disappear
why hope for things as they are not
why fear the only reality there is
        and the wall remains flat

I face the wall
to accept my reflection
breath by breath I count
tranquility alive in life dramas
as surely as
        the wall remains flat

NORTH DAKOTA

To be in the lap
  of the female One
Is to be in North Dakota,
Driving along her skirt
  how wide and lumpy
Her lap is!
Big enough for creatures
  Who like to eat all day
  from horizon to horizon

Green is the color
  of her skirt
With a blanket
  of soft white cotton
Held just above us –
  in case we might get cold,
When we creatures need to rest

The miles continue,
  on and on we go
Driving in North Dakota
  and the day grows old
Tired and hungry,
No worries
  for we are still in
The endless lap of God

MASSAGE SIGHT/SITE

Massage revels
new awareness
to be in the body
discover it is good
by looking in
instead of looking out
a view of soft water colors
that flow together
in my muscle caves,
not the primary colors
of mental objectivity
that tax the body
Massage, how sweet!
I love it
it relaxes me
Mind, body, spirit
Singing together
while all the colors
Mix
Blend
Melt
into
pure whiteness
of
Lightness

RED HOT ENDING

This morning at daybreak
I open the shutters to
See the sky,
      Behold
a giant dark cloud
thick and fierce like a
Big black bull
stomping down on a
Tiny sliver of light
      Crushed
unable to rise

So obvious ominous
I reject it
this image
Not like any part of my life
      No!
just a black cloud
Go back to bed
Close your eyes
Block it out and rest,
      I tried
but soon got up
to see the sky again

It can't be true!

The black bull
blown and stretched
into gray party streamers
        Waving harmlessly as
the red-orange balloon
Takes center stage
in the spreading backdrop
Of light
It glows out into the world
in joyful glory,
Ready to party ---
a sensation I observe
but do not feel
For behold
        when I shut out
the terror of the beginning
I am uninitiated and
        unprepared
to jump into
        The red hot ending

we all have
hard parts in
life – the author
is telling the
reader that
these are
important to
appreciate the
good.

37

DARK NIGHT OF THE SOUL

It's not easy to write about dark night
when the soul journeys to a terrible place
you didn't know existed
but its location is so close
too close!
You don't get to choose to go or not
the soul takes this leap
under its own power
with strong divine approval,
You only know it's there
when you arrive
and all the lights go out,
surrounded by nothing
you care about
You have entered
the inner wasteland

What can I say about its bare landscape
where all our props disappear
that comfort us in the outer world
and gave us real identity
Here the soul has nothing solid
to support it
Or cheer it up
and everything tastes like sand

Only a fool gives advice
In this dark night of the soul
where guidance comes from
a different source and
the soul will discover it
with its own process of time,
But once in my poverty
I felt a sadness
so intense and engulfing
not for me but
for the wasteland
It stirred a maternal instinct
and I hummed a little tune
that something might grow
In this forsaken sand
and I felt a drop of water
on my face

And I knew then
my soul would journey
        onward
and dark night would flow into
A new day
        unwritten

TWO COYOTES

A dusting of snow early
  In north Texas
Weird white
  Amidst autumn brown,
From nowhere two coyotes
  Stand in the open urban landscape
Beside highway 26
  Where do you belong?
I speed by
  Following the traffic
I glimpse your head
  Held high and bright eyes
Looking past the cars
  To the wild tangle
Of vines and brush
  Along the railroad track
On the opposite side of 26,
  In my side mirror
I see the two forms
  Begin to move into the highway
I gasp in fear
  No, you don't belong!
Then I sense a rhythm
  In your graceful gaits
That parallels the traffic
  And the two flow together

Across the 4 lanes
  Without a single red brake light,
I breathe again

Where do you belong?
  Who are you?
Could you be Coyote,
  The trickster of native folklore
Showing yourself today
  Master of both sides
Of highway 26
  No worries about which side
And the resourceful animal
  Who traverses worlds
Without a scratch and
  Just for the pure fun of it
Travels with a friend
  Yes, Coyote, I'm impressed
If I could learn your ways!

WINGS AT 50

I didn't notice but
since I turned 50
I've been folding up
my butterfly wings
little by little
until one day
I find myself alone
        In a tight cocoon

My bright yellows that soar
and fun polka dots
that glitter
in the morning light
shut down,
closed for the season,
        No vacancy!

Where did fluttering go?
garden bouquets inspiring
somersaults and long
summer lunches with friends
traveling here and there ---
the lure of exploring the new
        Where did fluttering go?

My cocoon holds me

still as a stone
my eyes have turned
away from the sun
I stare backwards
layer upon layer
memory after memory
pull me deeper
   Into the cocoon

Is this it?
   The future is my past
     No new colors!
      Ever

Can I be trusting
can I be stillness
until this cocoon
breaks open
Can I? Will I?
   If so,
My next new wings
   perhaps revealing the
Color of mystery
   the beauty of endurance
     the design of emptiness
Layered with all the Loves
    I've known
   My wings at 50

THE EMPTY CHAIR

The empty chair miracle
Of long ago
Lost count of the years
But not the power
Of the unexpected
Entering my life
Through the unnoticed
Insignificant place
Where my ego doesn't reign
Like an empty chair
A holy messenger can slip in
Under my guards
Announcing Good News
Of love and friendship,
The second miracle
Of the empty chair
We listened!
And we left gifted
With Grace and Glory
That gives hope
For the empty chairs
We bump into daily

I STAND IN THE BACKYARD

I stand in the backyard
my eyes closed
Inhale a deep, deep belly-breath
I smell pine trees
and sweet white jasmine
plus a scent of recent mowed grass
mixed with crushed oak leaves,
I inhale another breath
Filling my chest
With the fresh fragrance of God
Holy
Holy Holy

I love this smell!

↳ I imagine this as the smell after the rain. Love it!

45

ONE BIG TABLE

Above the Little River tonight
the Big Dipper hangs upside down
like our Thanksgiving gravy ladle
Our son used today to spoon
Creamy homemade giblet gravy
over the half-plate size serving of
Southern cornbread dressing
before passing it to his Dad
Then his grandparents
Waiting their turn
at ages 85 and 92,
Together as a family thankful
for this moment in time
The 5 of us around the table
Eating and talking
with our mouths full
and missing
sister, brother-in-law and
the young family of 3
who live across the ocean and already
living into tomorrow (their time),
I'll Skype with them tomorrow (my time)
and ask
did they notice the
Big Dipper too
and how it seems
The world is one big table

Receiving unknown
delicious
ladles full of extravagance
Spooned or dipped out
Whether we realize it or not
for this
we lift up our hands
In praise

TO ME AND THE SEA

I am sailing
In the ocean of Oneness
And my heart sings
In the air so sweet
     Without any effort
I keep sailing
In the ocean of Oneness
Breathing is simple
     The air breathes me
And the result is singing
     The song of the heart
As it flows undivided
Without censor
Out into the wind and sea

     Unlike sailing
In the waters of fantasy
Where the ride bounces
On the crescent rolling waves
     Screams of excitement
     As we crash into the trough
     Spray-soaked we rise again
For the next surging wave
Hoping it will be bigger
And lift us higher,
     We yell in glee

I am sailing
        in the ocean of Oneness
        how far from my harbor
                I trust you sail too
                In this air so sweet,
and if your heart fills
as you glide along
        Where the wind
        Breathes you alive
                Without any strain
                        Open your mouth
                        and let the love song
                                Sing free ---
                                To me and the sea

MOM MUST SEE DAUGHTER

There are times
When a Mom must see
   her daughter
No matter what!

I board the small RJ
With 10 other brave souls
   who like me
Defy Hurricane Irene

Off we lift
Racing Irene up the coast
Giant grey wall cloud
 to the east
Soon answers back

The pilot flies like he's driving
Moonshine through the mountains
   back in Tennessee
Bouncing on a washboard basin road
My teeth chattering

Lord, am I a fool
MLK monument dedication
   cancelled in DC
But there are times

When a Mom must see
   Her daughter

We zigzag towards D.C.
With that mean wall cloud
   glaring next to us
"Who do you think you are?"

This pilot takes on the challenge
Gas petal floored
Little engine squalling
   No turning back now,
just ride the bumps, ignore the dips!

We start going downhill
I feel the brake on the slippery gravel
   We're going down!
Nose against the window
I see the Potomac under the wing,
The pilot aims it hard to the ground
   Big bounce and I'm in D.C.!

No, can't worry about disasters around here
   Today or tomorrow
Truth is
   there are times
When a Mom must see
   her daughter
And I will!

SISSY OUR CAT

(El Dia de los Muertos)

Are you born a little kitty today
Or are you sleeping in Jesus's arms,
Maybe stretched out along Mary's thighs
Purring out your love song,
Perhaps you are hiding
Under the big golden throne
Sassing at even holy hands
That might entrap you
But if no one tries to grab
You will leap softly
Onto the body
While we sleep
Kneading and singing
Contentment
Into stubborn flesh
Call it alive
To feel tenderness
Feminine tenderness
Pink and white,
Wherever you are today
Thank you for coming
To live with us
We will not forget
Your love song
Sweet Sissy

WILDNESS OF GOD

The thunderstorm threw water
Against the window all day
And poured more across the yard
But when I saw the river
      lifted up
Into the arms of the trees
I couldn't wait any longer

Like a child
I left the window
      to run out into the storm
Where the river flows up in the trees
To see the wildness of God

There each tree bending over
      hanging onto the runaway river
Tree arms stretched so long and thin
      "Come back! Come back!"
But the river never looked back

Other trees upriver
Long since dead and fallen
Laid to rest peacefully
      where they fell
Now these silent ones
      are picked up

To go where they do not
          wish to go
I see them coming down
Like spinning bumper cars
Hitting one another sideways
          then pushed out of sight

Next I see a hundred or more
Plastic water bottles
Where did they come from?
          Where will they go?
The wind spreads them
From bank to bank
          like guerrilla soldiers
Covering all the space
Some hiding in roots
          and behind boulders
Most marching onward

I look back at the house
It looks the same
But here everything is happening
Will it change the riverbank and
All that belongs to it
          Forever and ever
What does forever mean
          When I am standing in the
                Wildness of God?

DEER IN CADES COVE

Under a cold winter sky
a young buck grazes
As fog lifts like a white curtain
behind the trees to announce
This is a new day

The deer buck unaware
in this cove park paradise
Keeps nibbling brown weeds as we
focus our camera and   → This is me
Count his points (not impressive)

                    ↘ This is Jon!
Deer so familiar here
most ignore them
Searching instead for
a big bear, a fox or fierce bobcat
These are the exciting stories of Cades Cove

Soon the buck runs away
white tail held high like
A flag of surrender
we move on too
But later I ponder the deer buck
for I have read,
To such as this one
The Kingdom of heaven belongs!

EMBARRASSING WORD

Such an embarrassing word Jesus
for a female theology student
Open-minded and far too liberal
inclusive and ecumenical
Jesus, he's the wrong gender!

I tried hermeneutics of suspicion
until my mistrust led to Lilith
Who like me runs away
from divine men or tight places
And I was back at the start

Jesus, could he be a feminist
re-envision and re-imagine him
"Cosmic Christ" sounds cool
and soothing metaphorical theology
Friend, lover, mother?

More detours into liberation theology
critiques of crosses and violence
Jesus, was he a model of victimhood
they say Jesus means freedom
Or the word just drops out

When I walked into the chapel
I had forgotten the word

Not a rally cry, no more
or a feminist stance
Just plain tired of
the question-answer

No, I went to view the art
a life-size mosaic icon
Behind the altar
rough cut rocks and glass
With colors that strike together

I ran my hand across the icon
the stones like braille invite touch
Bewildering array of textures
and mingled with light
Reflects me back to me

I got a little carried away
climbed on top the priest's chair
Where he sits during mass
perhaps it was silly but
I wanted to touch the eyes

Even on the chair I couldn't
Reach the top of the cross
but on my tip-tip-toes
I put my hands over the
Sharp rocks of his crucified palm

Jesus and I looked almost eye to eye
our hands in a high-five clasp
Stretched bodies balancing on a chair
and on a cross
I don't know why ---
I kissed his lips

DROP BY DROP

I sit down by the waters
of the Little River
Knot of tension in my chest
Vision blurred
and I breathe out
a loud heavy sigh
like ice cracking
under a noonday sun
Expanding circle
Drop by drop
wet liquid
Moving past tension
Trapped in forms
no longer useful
I don't argue
Already I sense
a softness
Stronger than rigid ways
more air and water
Comfort my lungs
And I let go more

Now the physical me
is leading me
Deeper into solitude
brilliant thoughts can't achieve

Nor emotions of desire
this melting and breathing
Has its Source
in whirlwinds and glaciers
I faintly imagine
So I don't try
but breathe out
Once again
Air and water flowing
Washing my senses
And I'm slipping
Drop by drop
So silently
Into joy

COME INTO THE WORLD

Hey, hey Baby
I want to show you the blue, blue sky
The clouds are gone, the sun is warm
It's a good day to be born,
      Come, come into the world!

These Morning Glories on the fence
Pink and purple and white
They want to shine for you
      Come, come into the world today!

Look at these autumn trees
They are shaking with joy
In anticipation of you
      Come, come into the world!

A mist hangs over the river
God is bringing forth creation
In this wet river bottom this morning
      Come, come be a part of this day!

Your mom and dad ready
Their suitcases packed
And your tiny clothes laid out
      Come, come let's get moving

See what surprises
We your family has to show
And this wild land of earth and water
		We call out to you

And the little blue birdie hiding
In the willow tree sings out
Come, come into the world
		What a good, good day to be born!

Dedicated to Eleanor Teal Eklund,
	First Granddaughter

This poem reminds me of
when Lily was born and you
were there to hear her
first cries into the world!

TRIUNE ONE

Today on the bank of the Little River
something occurred
I can't explain
like a door opening from
an unknown world
Three otters swam through it
sleek, wet and shiny
aiming towards me
popping up close to the bank
then just as suddenly
as the door opened
it closed
Three otters dove
back into the unknown world
where they are probably
laughing and joking with each other
with flips, spins and spirals ---
games of delight

But this brief Visitation
opens the frontier
of my known world
changes how it feels
to be standing here
with mystery so close
doors appearing and

disappearing
right here
on the Little River
and oh, I'm glad
I don't pray
to a solitary God
But the Triune One

NATIVITY IN THE VALLEY

We humans inhabit
A sweet space between two worlds
      Earth and Sky
That can weave us strong
      or spin us crazy

The earth force Gaia who
      with golden fields of grain
flows in circles round,
      Birth, death and rebirth
Moving us through her cycles
Like a strong river current
  Surrounding us
      Driving us
          Always touching us

A high sky force
      seemingly disembodied
Shines out a path for us
a nice straight trajectory
      to propel us
          into tomorrow
Our progress
      points to our destiny
We view it, of course, as
High peak destination

Above the rest
Glorious --- worth the struggle!

These two forces
       Swirl together
Wherever we call home,
Whoever we are with,
Thus we are inspired
       deep in our bones
To find that sweet space
Throughout our life span
       to love and to work
Praying for Grace

But we find ourselves
       often confused
Just when we believe
We are nearing the top
A death comes and
       It looks like
Nativity in the valley
       Once again

COOING OF DOVES

At daybreak
The cooing of doves
Echoes the murmurs of prayers
voiced to the
Omnipresent Spirit
of God
in which we live and perish

The dove sings her song
and we bow our heads
At the breakfast table
for we are here!
Embodied creatures
Dependent on sky, water, fields
What is judged as cruel tragedy
The dove knows
Today
against all odds
Creation awakens
To sing out to
The blue Unknown
in freedom
rather than high hope
One more glorious time
and we at the breakfast table
Whisper

thank you
One more time
To thee

Made in the USA
Monee, IL
29 October 2022

16762540R00049